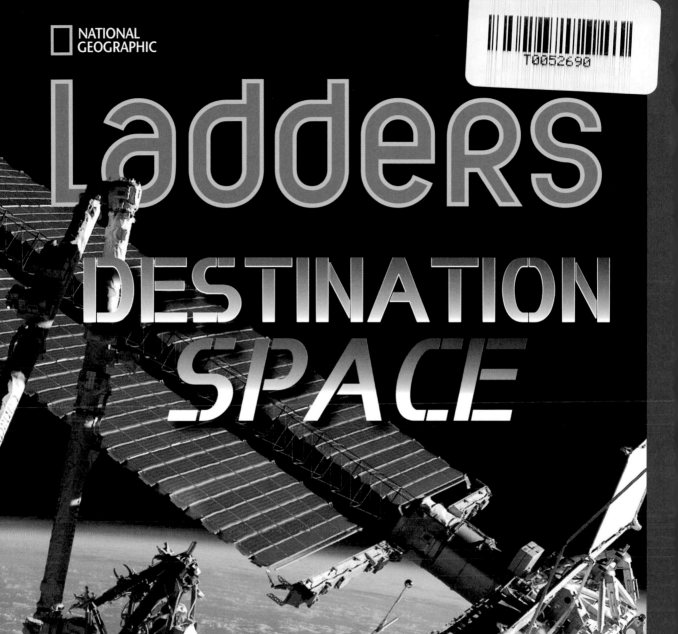

NATIONAL GEOGRAPHIC

Ladders

DESTINATION SPACE

Read to find out what it's like to travel into space.

BLAST OFF!

by Rebecca L. Johnson with Donald Thomas, astronaut

"I had been waiting for this moment since I was six years old. I was lying on my back, strapped inside my seat in the Space Shuttle Columbia. It was minutes before launch and my first trip into space. Six seconds before liftoff, the three main engines roared to life. My seat bucked. It rattled. It rolled. If I hadn't been strapped in, the rumbling would have tossed me to the floor. Columbia blasted skyward. Eight and half minutes later, everything went silent. The main engines shut down. I was in space."

Space Shuttle Columbia blasts off into space. Aboard are Don Thomas and his fellow astronauts.

DONALD A. THOMAS became an astronaut in 1991. Don flew four space shuttle missions from 1994–1997. He spent over 1,040 hours in space. That's about 43 days!

Don Thomas did what most people only dream of doing. He traveled into space. He flew in a space shuttle. A space shuttle flies faster and higher than an airplane. It flies so high that it goes into **orbit** around Earth.

What can you see from hundreds of miles above Earth? Join Don on his first space mission.

Don had a good view of the sun from the shuttle. The sun is a star. It looks bigger than other stars. That is because the sun is much closer to Earth than stars we see at night. The sun is a ball of gases. It gives off huge amounts of heat and light. The sun's energy warms Earth.

As Earth orbits the sun, it spins on its **axis.** Earth spins all the way around once every 24 hours. On Earth you can see one sunrise and one sunset every day. But the shuttle was traveling around Earth at 28,000 kilometers (17,500 miles) per hour. That's fast! So Don saw 16 sunrises and sunsets every day!

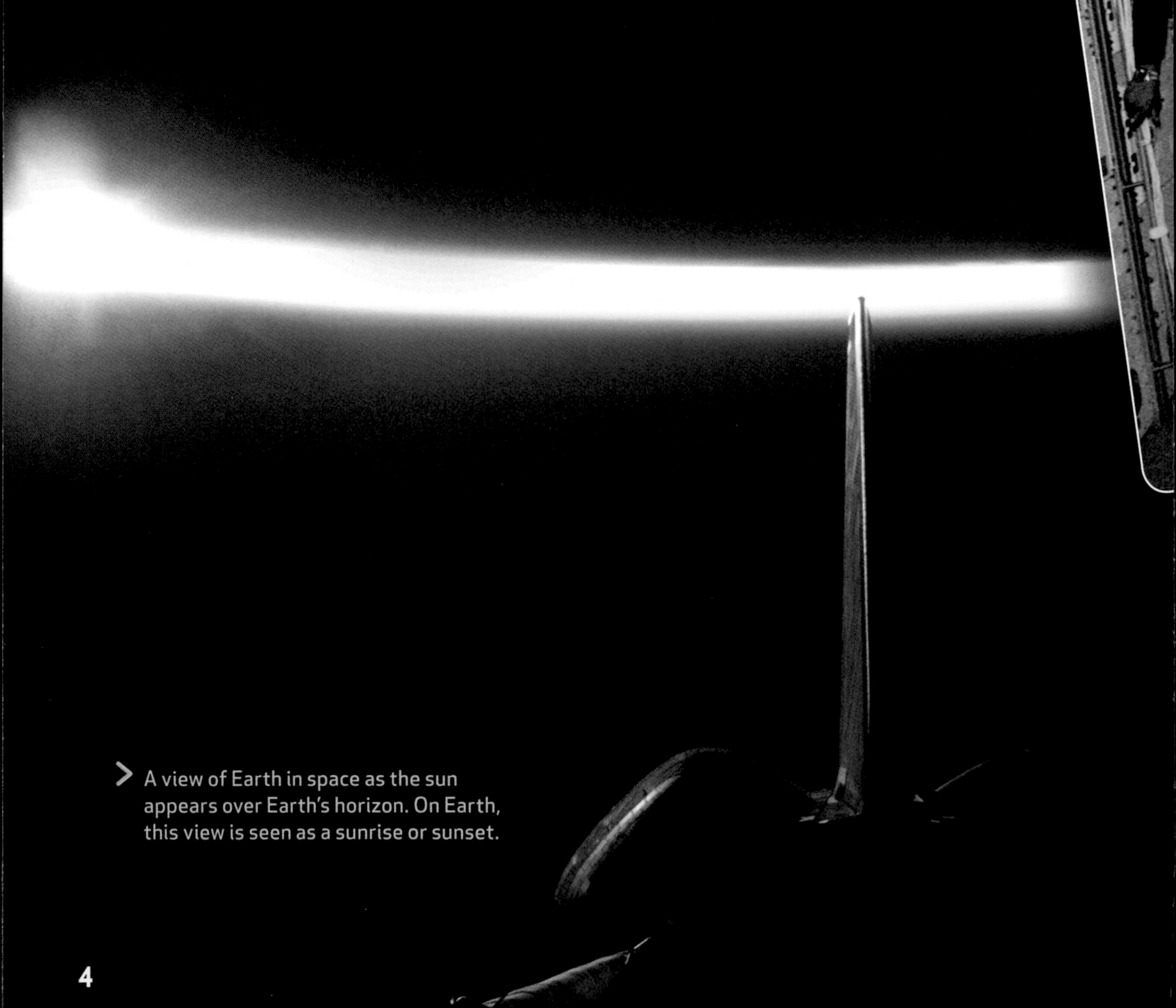

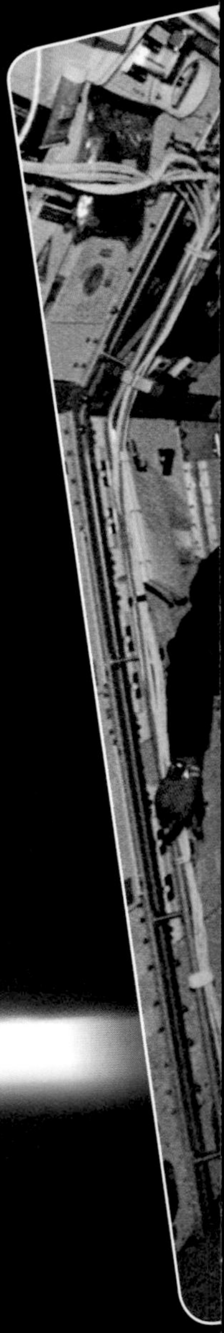

A view of Earth in space as the sun appears over Earth's horizon. On Earth, this view is seen as a sunrise or sunset.

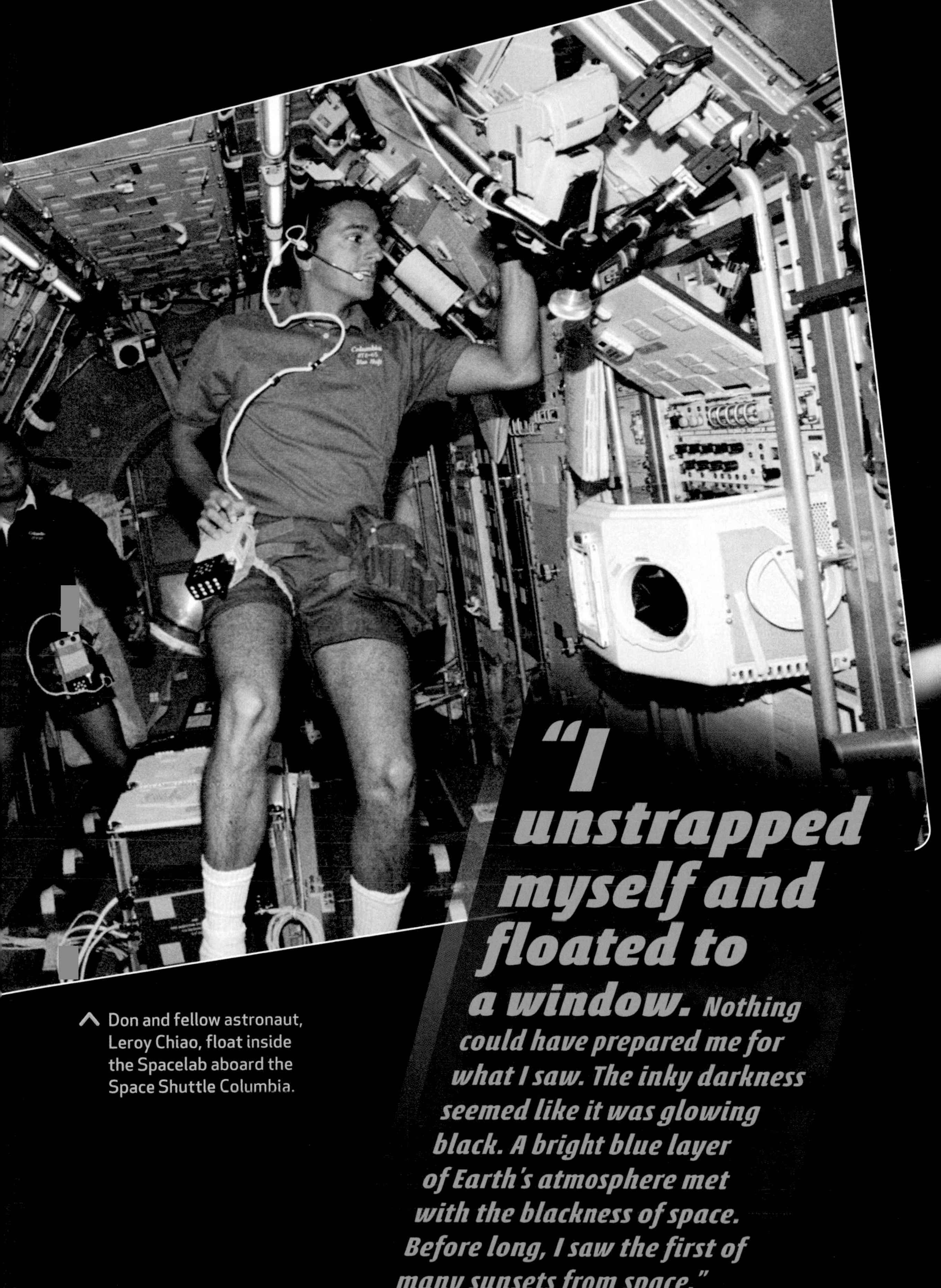

^ Don and fellow astronaut, Leroy Chiao, float inside the Spacelab aboard the Space Shuttle Columbia.

***"I unstrapped myself and floated to a window.** Nothing could have prepared me for what I saw. The inky darkness seemed like it was glowing black. A bright blue layer of Earth's atmosphere met with the blackness of space. Before long, I saw the first of many sunsets from space."*

Astronauts aboard space shuttles often view objects traveling through space. This comet was seen through windows of the Space Shuttle Columbia.

"From the space shuttle I could see many more stars than I could ever see from the ground. On Earth, the atmosphere blocks some of the light from each star. The atmosphere not only dims starlight, it changes how stars look. Moving gases in the atmosphere cause stars to twinkle. In space, stars don't twinkle. They look like steady points of light."

Aboard the Space Shuttle Columbia, Don works on an experiment designed to be done in space.

Stars come in different colors. Don saw white, blue, and red stars. He also saw yellow stars like the sun. The coolest stars are red. Warm stars are yellow. The hottest stars are blue.

Stars are in groups called **galaxies.** Our galaxy is called the Milky Way. It includes the sun and about 200 billion other stars.

Scientists think there are about 80–100 billion other galaxies in space.

A drag chute helps stop the Space Shuttle Columbia as it lands back on Earth.

"After staring at all the strange and wonderful sights in the night sky, it was good to see the old familiar sun once again. I soon realized that I was a little homesick. As amazing as stars and galaxies are, there's no place like Earth."

Don made three more trips into space. In 2011, the space shuttle program ended. The shuttles had flown 135 missions. What will the future of space travel be like? Will astronauts travel in super-fast rockets? Whatever happens, it's sure to be an amazing adventure!

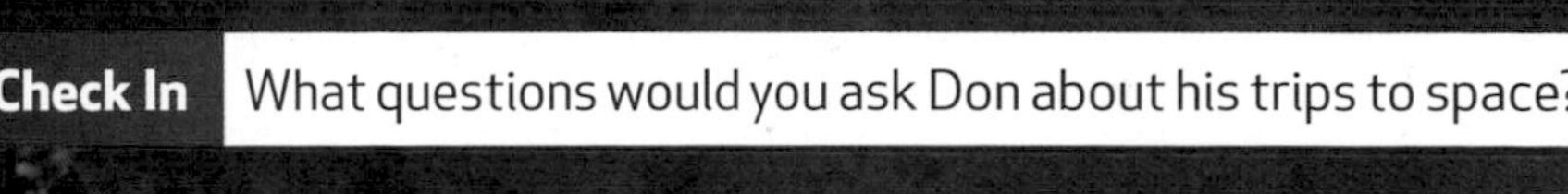
Check In What questions would you ask Don about his trips to space?

GENRE Reference Article | **Read to find out** about space telescopes.

Hubble and Beyond

by Rebecca L. Johnson

Many people use **telescopes** to look at stars. But telescopes on Earth make stars look blurry. That's because you have to look through Earth's atmosphere to see them. The key to seeing more of space would be putting telescopes above Earth's atmosphere.

So scientists invented telescopes that **orbit** in space.

Solar panels change sunlight into electricity. Electricity powers the Hubble Telescope.

Meet Hubble!

- The Hubble Space Telescope was launched in 1990. It is named after the astronomer Dr. Edwin Hubble.
- Hubble is as big as a school bus. It orbits Earth about 569 kilometers (353 miles) above Earth's surface.
- Hubble picks up visible light. It also picks up some light that human eyes cannot see.
- Hubble helps scientists make colorful pictures of stars and **galaxies.**
- Astronauts have improved Hubble since it was launched. It is now about 100 times more powerful.

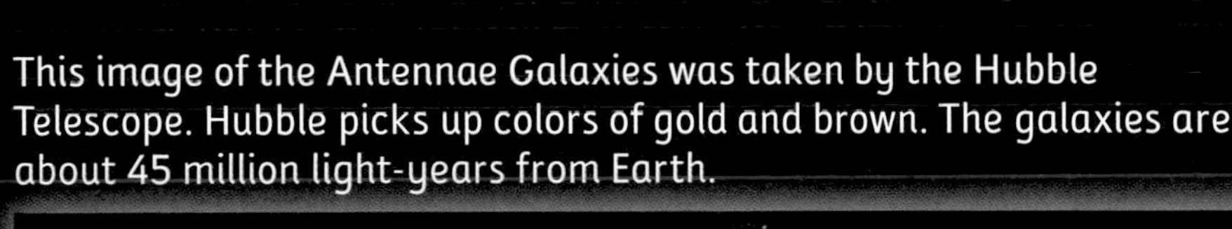

This image of the Antennae Galaxies was taken by the Hubble Telescope. Hubble picks up colors of gold and brown. The galaxies are about 45 million light-years from Earth.

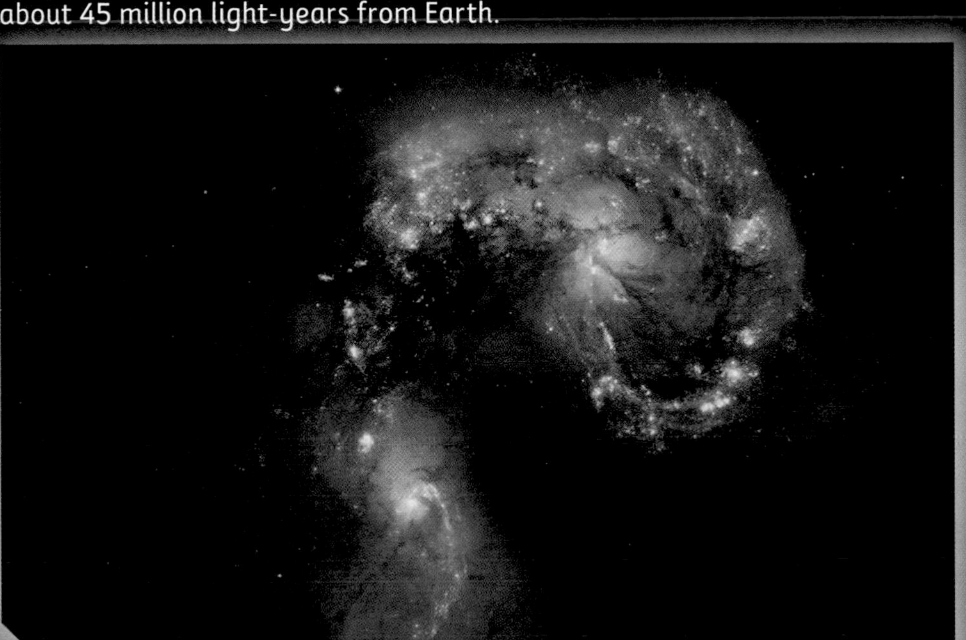

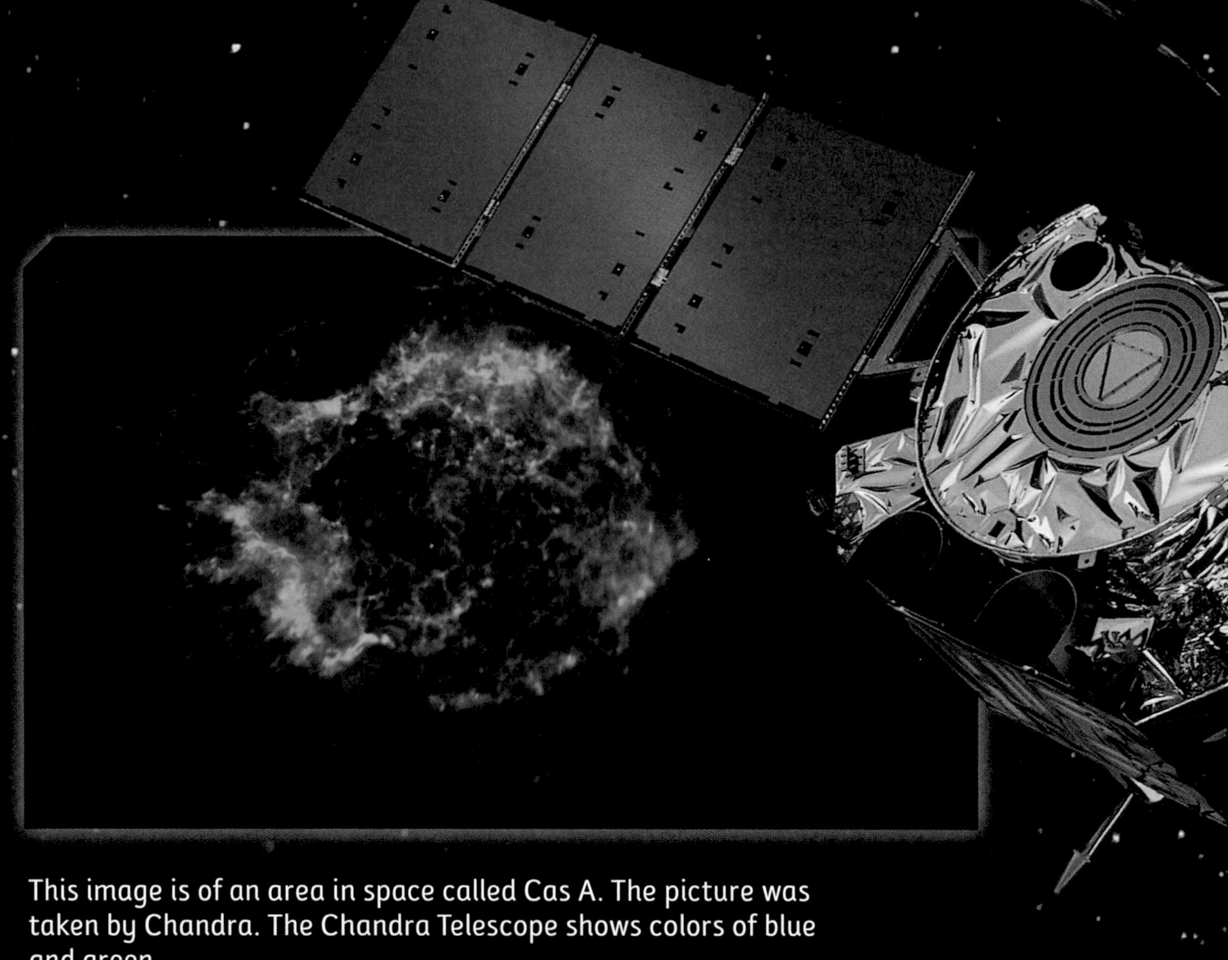

This image is of an area in space called Cas A. The picture was taken by Chandra. The Chandra Telescope shows colors of blue and green.

Introducing Chandra!

- **The Chandra X-ray Observatory is a space telescope. It was launched in 1999. It is named after space scientist Dr. Chandrasekhar.**
- **Chandra is about 14 meters (45 feet) long. That is longer than a school bus. It is one of the biggest telescopes in space.**
- **Chandra detects X-rays. X-rays are an invisible form of light. Hot objects give off X-rays.**
- **Scientists look at Chandra's images. They learn about exploding stars, hot gases, and black holes.**

The telescope has powerful thrusters. They help scientists move Chandra in space.

Solar panels turn sunlight into electricity. The electricity powers Chandra.

This is an artist's illustration of Chandra in space.

Amazing Spitzer!

- The Spitzer Space Telescope was launched in 2003. It is named after Dr. Lyman Spitzer, Jr. He first thought of putting large telescopes in space.
- Spitzer is about 4 meters (13 feet) long. It is about the size of a large van.
- Spitzer picks up only infrared light. People can't see this type of light. They feel infrared light as heat.
- Spitzer's images show scientists huge dust clouds, galaxies, and dying stars.

This image show a large star-forming area near the Milky Way. The red colors in it were picked up by the Spitzer Telescope.

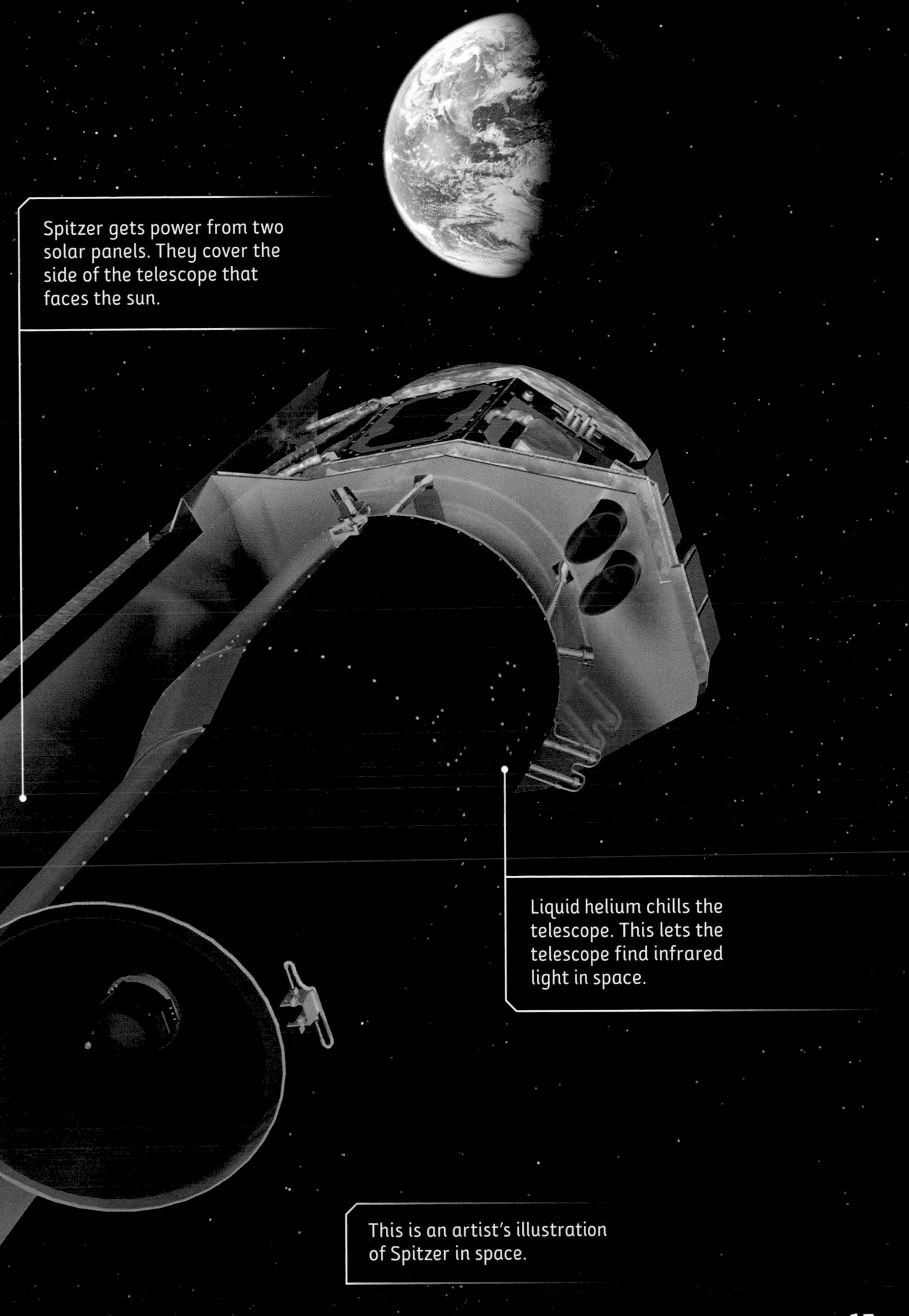

Spitzer gets power from two solar panels. They cover the side of the telescope that faces the sun.

Liquid helium chills the telescope. This lets the telescope find infrared light in space.

This is an artist's illustration of Spitzer in space.

Putting Them Together!

Each telescope takes different images. Each image gives scientists information. Scientists combine the images to learn more.

Galaxy M82 is about 12 million light-years from Earth. Scientists studied images of Galaxy M82. The images were taken by the Hubble, Chandra, and Spitzer Telescopes. Scientists learned that some new stars die in explosions called **supernovas.**

Scientists have learned a lot with space telescopes. Space telescopes help scientists see things they could not have seen from Earth. Space telescopes will help in making future discoveries.

Hubble's view of M82 shows a medium-sized galaxy. (See the green.) Hubble also detected hot gas coming out of the galaxy. (See the orange.)

Chandra detected X-rays. They come from super hot gases. They look like blue patches surrounding the galaxy.

This is a collection of images. They were taken from the Hubble, Chandra, and Spitzer Telescopes. Images from the telescopes are combined. They show an amazing view of starburst galaxy M82.

Spitzer's infrared view shows a huge cloud of gas and dust coming out of the galaxy's center. (See the red.)

Check In What information have scientists learned from space telescopes?

GENRE Third-Person Narrative

Read to find out what it's like to live in space.

LIVING IN SPACE

by Rebecca L. Johnson

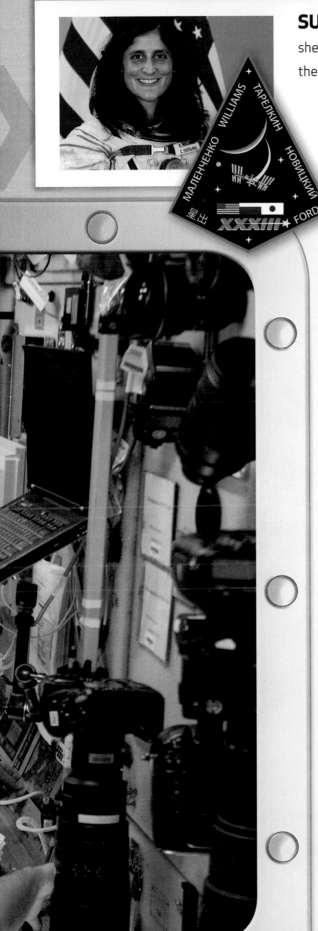

SUNITA WILLIAMS was a Navy jet pilot. Then she began astronaut training in 1998. She's been on the International Space Station twice.

Imagine blasting up into space. Now imagine living in **orbit** high above Earth for months.

Astronaut Sunita Williams has spent 322 days in space. Most of those days were on the International Space Station (ISS). The ISS orbits about 400 kilometers (250 miles) above Earth. In 2012, Sunita worked on the ISS with astronauts from Japan, Russia, and the United States.

What is it like to live on the ISS? "We are busy all the time," Sunita says. "Every day is a little bit different. It's awesome!"

Sunita wears a spacesuit to protect her while outside of the station. The reflective visor protects Sunita's eyes from the harmful rays of the sun.

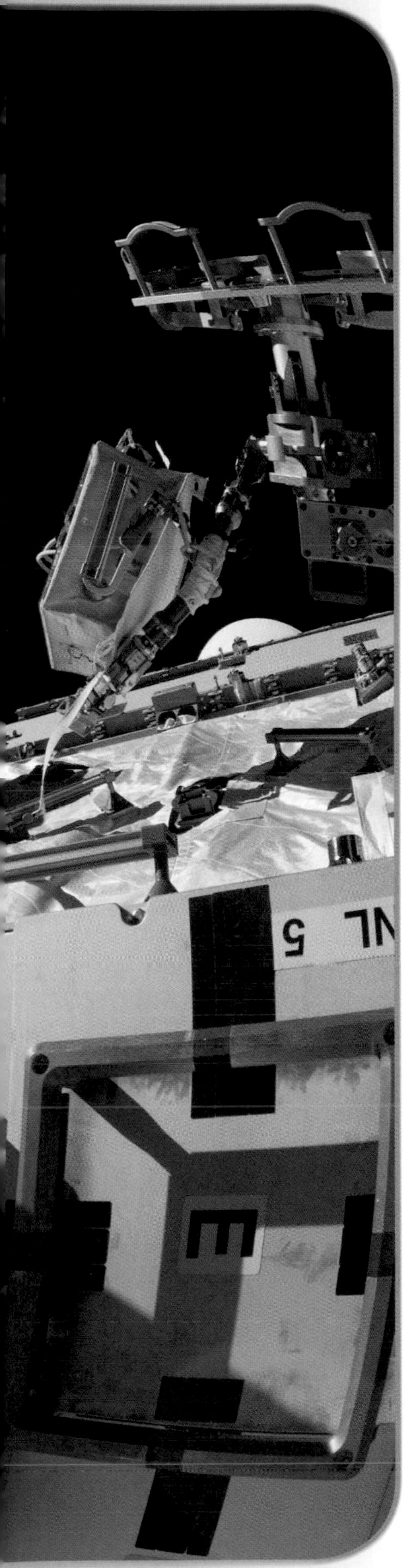

This image shows the ISS in space, with Earth far below.

Sunita spent most of her time inside the ISS. Sometimes she went outside to make small repairs.

Sunita has been on more spacewalks than any other woman. She has spent more than 50 hours outside the ISS in space.

"When you live in space, you feel weightless. And if something isn't tied down, it floats," Sunita says.

Astronauts put their gear in lockers. They strap things down. They hang onto straps or tuck their toes into footholds. When they want to move, they glide through the air from place to place.

There are lots of places to go in the ISS. The ISS is as large as a football field. It has as much space to live in as a five-bedroom house. There are science labs, two bathrooms, a gym, and lots of windows.

Living in space is hard work. But there's also time for relaxing. Sunita exercises in the gym every day. She talks to her family and friends on Earth. And sometimes she and the other astronauts watch videos.

One of Sunita's favorite pastimes is looking down at Earth. "It's just pretty. I mean, it's blue, it's green, it's purple. The clouds are forming, the ice is forming. It is just spectacular."

Sunita works with Robonaut 2 in a scientific investigation.

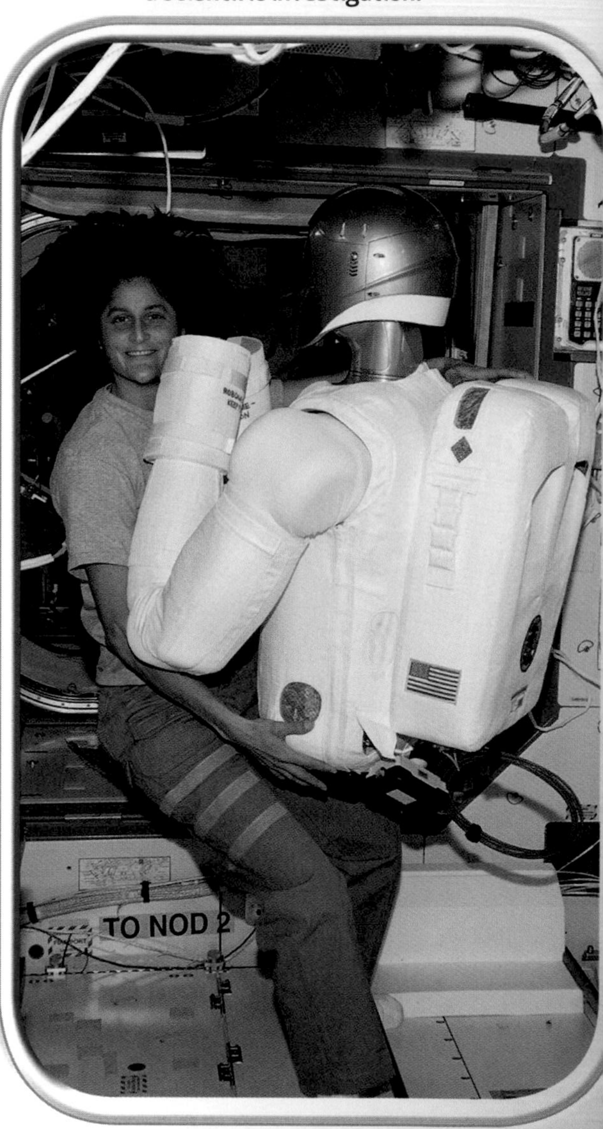

Sunita prepares a snack in the ISS kitchen.

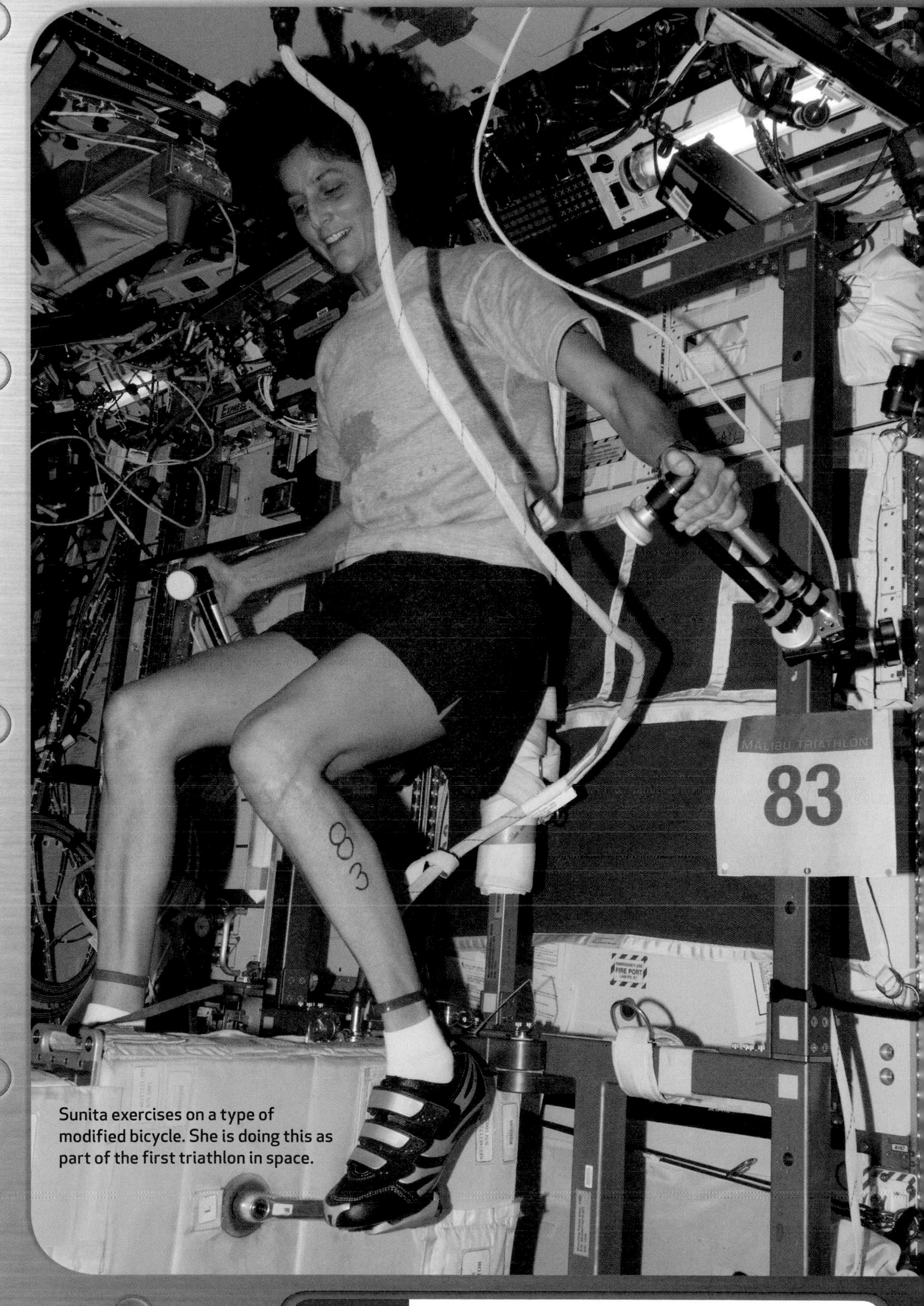

Sunita exercises on a type of modified bicycle. She is doing this as part of the first triathlon in space.

Check In What questions would you ask Sunita about the ISS?

Discuss

1. Compare the experiences Don Thomas had aboard the Shuttle Columbia with Sunita Williams's experiences aboard the ISS. How are they the same? How are they different?

2. Compare and contrast the different space telescopes in "Hubble and Beyond." Which do you think is the most interesting telescope? Explain your answer.

3. Would you like to travel to or live in space? Why or why not? Explain your answer.

4. NASA's shuttle program ended in 2012. What do you think is the future of space travel? Where could you look to find out more about space travel and space exploration?